FDA Quality System Requirements for
Medical Devices (21 CFR Part 820)

A Practitioner's Guide to Management
Controls

- 820.20, Management Responsibility
- 820.22, Quality Audit
- 820.25, Personnel

D.G.   Daugherty

ISBN: 1522840249
ISBN-13: 978-1522840244

DEDICATION

To Beth and Daniel.

CONTENTS

ACKNOWLEDGMENTS

Much of the material in this book has been extracted from U.S. Food and Drug Administration sources available at fda.gov as indicated in the book. I would like to sincerely thank my wife, Beth, for her patience and guidance during the development of the book.

1 INTRODUCTION

This book provides a practitioner's guide to the United States' Food and Drug Administration's (FDA) requirements for Management Controls as described in 21 CFR Part 820 Quality System Regulation (QS Regulation) for Medical Devices. Management Controls include sections 820.20 Management Responsibility, 820.22 Quality Audit, and 820.25 Personnel of this medical device regulation.

I wrote this *Practitioner's Guide to Management Controls* because it seems that many practitioners, particularly those new to medical devices, are sometimes overwhelmed by the QS Regulation requirements for management controls and how to interpret them. These practitioners may also not be aware of, or have access to, many of the resources available to many of us in the industry. Having experienced the same challenges at times in my twenty five year medical device career, I determined that I would provide a concise, comprehensive, and affordable, collection of information pertaining to the QS Regulation that may prove helpful to these practitioners.

I wrote the *Practitioner's Guide to Management Controls* to align with the FDAs top down inspection approach for quality subsystems documented in its Guide to Inspections of Quality Systems. This document is also known as the Quality System Inspection Technique (QSIT) Guide. Using this approach, the FDA believes that by focusing their inspection efforts on key elements of a firm's quality system it can more efficiently and effectively evaluate that quality system. This is in contrast to the bottom up inspection approach where the FDA may identify specific problems by reviewing nonconformance reports and working its way up to the system that handles non conformances. This bottom up approach is no longer considered by FDA as an efficient or effective approach in general because it takes more time and ultimately may not identify systemic issues as readily as the top down approach.

In the QSIT Guide, the FDA identifies four major subsystems in the quality system to evaluate when using this top down approach, namely, Management Controls; Corrective and Preventive Actions; Design Controls; and Production and Process Controls. The FDA also identifies three additional subsystems that are indirectly evaluated in a top down inspection. These subsystems are records/documents/change controls, facilities and equipment controls, and material controls.

The *Practitioner's Guide to Management Controls* was written to provide a simple, single source of information for practitioners particularly interested in the management controls subsystem. It is written for the practitioner to use as a tool to help develop management controls prospectively for a new quality system or to perform gap assessments between existing management controls in a quality system against the FDA requirements and expectations provided in this book.

The essential QS Regulation related information I include in the *Practitioner's Guide to Management Controls* comes directly from the following FDA sources:

- **Preamble to 21 CFR Part 820 Quality System Regulation for Medical Devices**: The preamble contains public comments received by the FDA during the development of the regulation and describes the FDAs resolution of the comments. The preamble provides some valuable information pertaining to FDA's intent of the regulation and expectations for firms in the medical device industry.

- **21 CFR Part 820 Quality System Regulation for Medical Devices**: This regulation defines the current good manufacturing practice (CGMP) requirements for finished medical devices. The requirements in this regulation govern the methods used in, and the facilities and controls used for, the design, manufacture, packaging, labeling, storage, installation, and servicing of all finished devices intended for human use. The requirements in this part are intended to ensure that finished devices will be safe and effective and otherwise in compliance with the United States' Federal Food, Drug, and Cosmetic Act.

- **FDA's Guide to Inspections of Quality Systems (QSIT Guide).** This document provides guidance to the FDA field staff on the inspectional process used to assess a medical device manufacturer's compliance with the Quality System Regulation and related regulations.

The inspectional process is known as the "Quality System Inspection Technique" or "QSIT".

- **Warning Letters.** A form of notification used by the FDA to firms when the FDA finds that a manufacturer has significantly violated FDA regulations. Warning Letters identify the violations and also makes clear that the firm must correct the problem. These letters also provide directions and a timeframe for the firm to inform FDA of its plans for correction. FDA then checks to ensure that the company's corrections are adequate. Samples of warning letters related to the requirement(s) issued to medical device companies for not meeting requirements in the QS Regulation are included in this book.

The requirements in the QS Regulation and the inspection objectives and techniques referenced from the QSIT Guide are directly quoted from those sources to assure the practitioner that the information comes directly from the FDA. Preamble comments are quoted directly (unless otherwise indicated) and the sample warning letters are paraphrased from the data in the FDA's warning letter database located at www.fda.gov.

The *Practitioner's Guide to Management Controls* is comprised of seven sections. Section one, this section, is an introduction to the book. Section two provides key terms from the QS Regulation that are important to know for understanding management controls. Section three provides a general overview of management controls. Sections four through six cover the following subject matter in detail: management responsibility, quality audit, and personnel. These sections include the applicable QS Regulation section, excerpts from the preamble, QSIT inspection techniques, and samples of warning letters. The information in each section should provide ample guidance for the practitioner to develop or improve management controls at their firm. Section seven is the book's conclusion.

Finally, please be reminded that the *Practitioner's Guide to Management Controls* is written for practitioners trying to better understand, implement, or improve management controls per the QS Regulation, not for requirements in other regulations or standards (e.g. ISO 13485). Though the requirements are most likely similar, the author suggests that guidance be obtained from other sources for meeting these other regulation and standard requirements.

2 KEY TERMS

These key terms are from Subpart A – General Provisions of the QS Regulation, sections 820.1 Scope and 820.3 Definitions

- 820.1 Scope (a) Applicability (3)

  - In this regulation the term "where appropriate" is used several times. When a requirement is qualified by "where appropriate," it is deemed to be "appropriate" unless the manufacturer can document justification otherwise. A requirement is "appropriate" if non implementation could reasonably be expected to result in the product not meeting its specified requirements or the manufacturer not being able to carry out any necessary corrective action.

- 820.3 Definitions

  - *Establish* means define, document (in writing or electronically), and implement.

- o *Management with executive responsibility* means those senior employees of a manufacturer who have the authority to establish or make changes to the manufacturer's quality policy and quality system.

- o *Manufacturer* means any person who designs, manufactures, fabricates, assembles, or processes a finished device. Manufacturer includes but is not limited to those who perform the functions of contract sterilization, installation, relabeling, remanufacturing, repacking, or specification development, and initial distributors of foreign entities performing these functions.

- o *Quality* means the totality of features and characteristics that bear on the ability of a device to satisfy fitness-for-use, including safety and performance.

- o *Quality policy* means the overall intentions and direction of a firm with respect to quality, as established by management with executive responsibility.

- o *Quality system* means the formal structure, responsibilities, procedures, processes, and resources for implementing quality management.

3 MANAGEMENT CONTROLS

According to the Quality System Inspection Technique Guide (QSIT), it is essential that the firm establishes and maintains a quality system that is appropriate for the specific medical device being manufactured and meets the requirements of the Quality System Regulation (QS Regulation). The management controls subsystem is expected to be established to ensure that this occurs at the firm.

In the QSIT, the purpose of the management control subsystem is to provide adequate resources for device design, manufacturing, quality assurance, distribution, installation, and servicing activities; assure the quality system is functioning properly; monitor the quality system; and make necessary adjustments. A quality system that has been implemented effectively and is monitored to identify and address problems is more likely to produce devices that function as intended.

So, when a Food and Drug Administration (FDA) inspection of the firm does occur, the primary purpose of conducting a management controls inspection is to determine whether management with executive responsibility ensures that an adequate and effective quality system has been established (defined, documented and implemented) at the firm. Because of this, the QSIT indicates that each inspection should begin and end with an evaluation of this subsystem.

Prior to the start of the inspection (if preannounced), the FDA may ask the firm to send their overall (or top level) quality system policies, objectives, and procedures. The firm should include their management review procedures, quality policy, and quality plan. If not requested prior to the start of the inspection, the FDA may review these documents at the start of the firm's inspection.

The firm must have a written quality policy. The definition of quality policy is provided in the QS Regulation. It means the overall intentions and directions of an organization with respect to quality. The firm is responsible for establishing a clear quality policy with achievable objectives, then translating the objectives into actual methods and procedures. Management with executive responsibility (i.e. has the authority to establish and make changes to the company quality policy) must assure the policy and objectives are understood and implemented at all levels of their organization. The policy does not need to be extensive. Personnel are not required to be able to recite the policy but they should be familiar with it and know where to obtain it.

Management reviews and quality audits are a foundation of a good quality system and must be conducted in a controlled manner. Firms must have written procedures for conducting management reviews and quality audits each must have defined intervals for when they should occur.

The firm's quality audits should examine the quality system activities to demonstrate that the procedures are appropriate to achieve quality system objectives, and the procedures have been implemented. A successful implementation of the firm's procedures should result in the firm achieving its quality policy and associated objectives. Whether the quality policy and objectives are "good" may become evident as the other subsystems are reviewed during the inspection.

The firm must have a written quality plan that defines the quality practices, resources and activities relevant to the devices that are being designed and manufactured at that facility. The firm needs to have written procedures that describe how they intend to meet their quality requirements.

For firms that manufacture devices as well as other products, there must be a quality plan that is specifically relevant to devices. Much of what is required to be part of the plan may be found in the firm's quality system documentation, such as, the Quality Manual, Device Master Record(s), production procedures, etc. Therefore, the plan itself may be a roadmap of the firm's quality system. The plan in this case would need to include reference to applicable quality system documents and how those documents apply to the device(s) that is the subject of the plan. Quality plans may be specific to one device or be generic to all devices manufactured at the firm. Quality plans can also be specific to processes or overall systems.

All manufacturers of medical devices are required to establish and implement a quality system tailored to the device manufactured. Each manufacturer must prepare and implement all activities, including, but not necessarily limited to the applicable requirements of the QS Regulation, that are necessary to assure the finished device, the design process, the manufacturing process, and all related activities conform to approved specifications.

The term "quality system" as specified in the QS Regulation includes assuring manufacturing processes are controlled and adequate for their intended use, documentation is controlled and maintained, equipment is calibrated, inspected, tested, etc. Some manufacturers may use the terms "quality control" or "GMP Control" or "quality assurance" instead of quality system. It doesn't matter what term is used as long as the quality system concept is understood and implemented.

The management controls subsystem is contained in Subpart B – Quality System Requirements, of the QS Regulation, and includes the following sections (and subsections).

- 820.20 Management Responsibility

  (a) Quality Policy
  (b) Organization
  (c) Management Review
  (d) Quality Planning
  (e) Quality System Procedures

- 820.22 Quality Audit, which includes requirements for an audit procedure, scheduling, execution, reporting, and follow ups to audits.

- 820.25 Personnel

A review of the FDA's warning letter database does suggest that firm's do have opportunities for improvement with establishing and maintaining management controls. Some issues include:

- Failure to establish and maintain procedures
- Failure to execute required procedures
- Failure to maintain or provide objective evidence demonstrating compliance to documented procedures

Careful review of the QS Regulation, Preamble, QSIT, and warning letters such as these may help a practitioner obtain a better understanding of what the FDA expects and how to develop and implement an effective quality system.

4 MANAGEMENT RESPONSIBILITY

THE REGULATION

Subpart B—Quality System Requirements

820.20 Management responsibility.

(a) Quality policy. Management with executive responsibility shall establish its policy and objectives for, and commitment to, quality. Management with executive responsibility shall ensure that the quality policy is understood, implemented, and maintained at all levels of the organization.

(b) Organization. Each manufacturer shall establish and maintain an adequate organizational structure to ensure that devices are designed and produced in accordance with the requirements of this part.

    (1)   Responsibility and authority. Each manufacturer shall establish the appropriate responsibility, authority, and interrelation of all personnel who manage, perform, and assess work affecting quality, and provide the independence and authority necessary to

perform these tasks.

(2) Resources. Each manufacturer shall provide adequate resources, including the assignment of trained personnel, for management, performance of work, and assessment activities, including internal quality audits, to meet the requirements of this part.

(3) Management representative. Management with executive responsibility shall appoint, and document such appointment of, a member of management who, irrespective of other responsibilities, shall have established authority over and responsibility for:

(i) Ensuring that quality system requirements are effectively established and effectively maintained in accordance with this part; and

(ii) Reporting on the performance of the quality system to management with executive responsibility for review.

(c) Management review. Management with executive responsibility shall review the suitability and effectiveness of the quality system at defined intervals and with sufficient frequency according to established procedures to ensure that the quality system satisfies the requirements of this part and the manufacturer's established quality policy and objectives. The dates and results of quality system reviews shall be documented.

(d) Quality planning. Each manufacturer shall establish a quality plan which defines the quality practices, resources, and activities relevant to devices that are designed and manufactured. The manufacturer shall establish how the requirements for quality will be met.

(e) Quality system procedures. Each manufacturer shall establish quality system procedures and instructions. An outline of the structure of the documentation used in the quality system shall be established where appropriate.

EXCERPTS FROM THE PREAMBLE

Management with executive responsibility is that level of management that has the authority to establish and make changes to the company quality policy. The establishment of quality objectives, the translation of such objectives into actual methods and procedures, and the implementation of the quality system may be delegated. The regulation does not prohibit the delegation. However, it is the responsibility of the highest level of management to establish the quality policy and to ensure that it is followed.

It is without question management's responsibility to undertake appropriate actions to ensure that employees

understand management's policies and objectives.
Understanding is a learning process achieved through
training and reinforcement. Management reinforces
understanding of policies and objectives by demonstrating
a commitment to the quality system visibly and actively on
a continuous basis. Such commitment can be demonstrated
by providing adequate resources and training to support
quality system development and implementation.

The requirement for "sufficient personnel" is covered in
section 820.20(b) (2), "Resources," and 820.25 Personnel,
both of which require manufacturers to employ sufficient
personnel with the training and experience necessary to
carry out their assigned activities properly.

FDA has retained the requirement for establishing an
"adequate organizational structure" to ensure compliance
with the regulation, because such an organizational
structure is fundamental to a manufacturer's ability to
produce safe and effective devices.

The organizational structure should ensure that the
technical, administrative, and human factors functions
affecting the quality of the device will be controlled,
whether these functions involve hardware, software,
processed materials, or services. All such control should be
oriented towards the reduction, elimination, or ideally,
prevention of quality nonconformities.

The organizational structure established will be determined
in part by the type of device produced, the manufacturer's

organizational goals, and the expectations and needs of customers. What may be an "adequate" organizational structure for manufacturing a relatively simple device may not be "adequate" for the production of a more complex device.

FDA has retained the broad requirement that the necessary independence and authority be provided as appropriate to every function affecting quality.

FDA emphasizes that it is crucial to the success of the quality system for the manufacturer to ensure that responsibility, authority, and organizational freedom (or independence) is provided to those who initiate action to prevent nonconformities, identify and document quality problems, initiate, recommend, provide, and verify solutions to quality problems, and direct or control further processing, delivery, or installation of nonconforming product.

Organizational freedom or independence does not necessarily require a stand-alone group, but responsibility, authority, and independence should be sufficient to attain the assigned quality objectives with the desired efficiency.

There is a broad requirement that the manufacturer provide adequate resources for the quality system and is not restricted to the verification function. FDA acknowledges that 820.25(a), "General," requires that sufficiently trained personnel be employed. However, 820.20(b) (2),

"Resources," emphasizes that all resource needs must be provided for, including monetary, supplies, etc., as well as personnel resources. In contrast, 820.25(a) specifically addresses education, background, training, and experience requirements for personnel

"Management representative," The agency agrees that the responsibility need not be assigned to "executive" management and has modified the requirement to allow management with executive responsibility to appoint a member of management. When a member of management is appointed to this function, potential conflicts of interest should be examined to ensure that the effectiveness of the quality system is not compromised. In addition the appointment of this person must be documented.

Instructions and procedures must be defined, documented, implemented, and maintained in such a way that the requirements of this part are met. If they are, they will be "effective.'

FDA will not request to inspect and copy the reports of reviews required by 820.20(c) when conducting routine inspections to determine compliance with this part. FDA believes that refraining from routinely reviewing these reports may help ensure that the audits are complete and candid and of maximum use to the manufacturer.

FDA believes that it is important that the dates and results of quality system reviews be documented, and FDA may require that management with executive responsibility certify in writing that the manufacturer has complied with the requirements of 820.20(c). FDA will also review the written procedures required by 820.20(c), as well as all other records required under 820.20. 52.

FDA believes that a manufacturer can establish procedures flexible enough for management to vary the way in which a review is conducted, as appropriate. Procedures should require that the review be conducted at appropriate intervals and should be designed to ensure that all parts of the quality system are adequately reviewed. A manufacturer may, of course, develop procedures that permit review of different areas at different times, so long as such reviews are sufficient to carry out the objectives of this section. If there are known problems, for example, a "sufficient frequency" may be fairly frequent. Further, because FDA will not be reviewing the results of such reviews, FDA must be assured that this function will occur in a consistent manner.

The purpose of the management reviews required by 820.20(c) is to determine if the manufacturer's quality policy and quality objectives are being met, and to ensure the continued suitability and effectiveness of the quality system. An evaluation of the findings of internal and supplier audits should be included in the 820.20(c) evaluation. The management review may include a review of the following: (1) The organizational structure, including the adequacy of staffing and resources; (2) the quality of the finished device in relation to the quality objectives; (3)

combined information based on purchaser feedback, internal feedback (such as results of internal audits), process performance, product (including servicing) performance, among other things; and (4) internal audit results and corrective and preventive actions taken.

Management reviews should include considerations for updating the quality system in relation to changes brought about by new technologies, quality concepts, market strategies, and other social or environmental conditions. Management should also review periodically the appropriateness of the review frequency, based on the findings of previous reviews. The quality system review process in 820.20(c), and the reasons for the review, should be understood by the organization.

FDA believes that outlining the structure of the documentation is beneficial and, at times, may be critical to the effective operation of the quality system. FDA recognizes, however, that it may not be necessary to create an outline in all cases. For example, it may not be necessary for smaller manufacturers and manufacturers of less complicated devices. Thus, the outline is only required where appropriate.

THE QSIT GUIDE

Inspectional Objectives

1. **Verify that a quality policy, management review and quality audit procedures, quality plan, and quality system procedures and instructions have**

been defined and documented.

Prior to the start of an inspection (if preannounced), the FDA will ask the firm to send their overall (or top level) quality system policies, objectives, and procedures. This should include their management review procedures, quality policy, and quality plan. If not received prior to the start of the inspection, the FDA will likely review these documents at the start of your inspection.

The FDA wants to determine that a firm has a written quality policy consistent with the definition of a quality policy in the QS Regulation. The quality policy must be established and include achievable objectives then translating the objectives into actual methods and procedures. Management with executive responsibility must assure the policy and objectives are understood and implemented at all levels of their organization. The policy does not need to be extensive. Personnel are not required to be able to recite the policy but they should be familiar with it and know where to obtain it.

2. Verify that a quality policy and objectives have been implemented.

One way the FDA uses to determine whether personnel are familiar with the quality policy is to ask employees directly. This is not typically done when an employee is engaged in the actual performance of his/her duties, but could be done when he/ she is at break or when he/she has finished a task and before he/she begins his/her next task.

FDA also looks to see how management has made the policy available. For example: Is it in their Quality Manual or another part of their written procedures? Is it posted at points throughout the building? It doesn't matter how a firm makes the policy known, only that personnel know that there is a policy and where they can read the policy for themselves.

A review of employee training records to show they have been trained in the firm's quality policy and objectives may also be done. In particular, this is likely to be done for those employees involved in key operations.

3. **Review the firm's established organizational structure to confirm that it includes provisions for responsibilities, authorities and necessary resources.**

A firm's organizational structure must be adequate to ensure devices are designed and manufactured in accordance with the QS Regulation. The organizational structure should ensure the technical, administrative, and human factors functions affecting the quality of a device are controlled. These functions may involve hardware, software, processed materials or services. All such control should be towards the reduction, elimination, or ideally, the prevention of quality nonconformities.

To determine what the firm's organizational structure is, the FDA may start by asking the authority and responsibility questions that are the start of every FDA inspection. They will also likely review the firm's organizational charts.

The firm's procedures should describe the functional areas or people responsible for performing certain tasks governed by their quality system. They should also include provisions for resources and designating a management representative.

The FDA will undertake to determine whether personnel involved in managing, performing or assessing work affecting quality have the necessary independence and authority to perform those tasks. Organizational freedom or independence does not necessarily require a stand-alone group. However, the responsibility, authority and independence should be sufficient to attain the firm's stated quality objectives.

Adequate resources must be available for the quality system to assure the firm's stated quality objectives can be achieved. Resources include money, supplies, personnel, etc. One approach to confirm that adequate resources are available is to ask the management representative how resources are obtained and allocated.

4.0   Confirm that a management representative has been appointed. Evaluate the purview of the

management representative.

The firm must appoint a management representative who is responsible for ensuring the quality system is effectively established and maintained, and who will report on its performance to management with executive responsibility for review. The appointment must be documented.

To determine whether there is in fact a documented management representative, the FDA will review the firm's organizational chart(s) or their Quality Manual.

The FDA will determine whether the appointed management representative actually has the purported responsibility and authority granted to him/her by the firm's procedures or organizational structure. Ways of reaching this determination include: Whether he/she has sign-off authority for changes to documents, processes, or product designs; whether the people conducting quality audits report or provide him/her with their results; and noting how he/she interacts with corrective and preventive actions, relative design control issues, complaints, MDRs, in-process or finished product failures, etc. In other words, his /her responsibility and authority should be apparent through the review of the other subsystems.

The FDA will verify that the management representative

is reporting back to the management with executive responsibility on the performance of the quality system. These reports should either be the subject of the management reviews or at least provide the framework for those reviews. NOTE: The agency's policy relative to the review of quality audit results is stated in CPG 7151.02 (CPG Manual subchapter 130.300). This policy prohibits FDA access to a firm's audit results. Under the QS Regulation, this prohibition extends to reviews of supplier audit reports and management reviews. However, the procedures and documents that show conformance with 21 CFR 820.50, Purchasing Controls, and 21 CFR 820.20(3)(c), Management Reviews, and 21 CFR 920.22 Quality Audit, are subject to FDA inspection.

5.0   Verify that management reviews, including a review of the suitability and effectiveness of the quality system, are being conducted.

Management reviews must measure the firm's quality system against the QS Regulation and the firm's own stated quality objectives as defined in their quality policy. Management reviews must be documented. There must be written procedures for conducting management reviews. These procedures can be inspected and the firm must certify in writing, if requested, that the firm has complied with this Quality System Regulation requirement.

FDA reviews the firm's management review schedule to confirm management reviews are being conducted with sufficient frequency. Management reviews should be frequent enough to keep them informed of ongoing quality issues and problems. During the review of the CAPA subsystem, if FDA finds that there are quality issues that do not seem to be known to executive-level management, then the reviews may not be occurring with sufficient frequency.

The dates and results of management reviews must be documented to show dates conducted and whether management with executive responsibility attended the reviews. It is not permissible as explained above for an FDA Investigator to review the firm's actual management review documentation. However, the firm should be able to show the FDA how the reviews are to be documented. Management review procedures or instructions should include a requirement that the results of the reviews be documented and dated.

6.0   Evaluate whether management with executive responsibility ensures that an adequate and effective quality system has been established and maintained.

At this point in an inspection, FDA may stop the review of the management system. The FDA will continue the inspection by evaluating the other subsystems. From their review of the other subsystems, FDA may determine if what they are finding indicates that management is appropriately carrying out responsibilities for providing adequate resources and overseeing the quality system to detect problems and address them.

This review may give FDA a better idea on whether the management representative has the appropriate authority and responsibility, whether the organizational structure is adequate, whether the quality audits and management reviews are sufficient, whether the quality policy has really been implemented, and whether the training being provided is sufficient.

A firm must have a written quality plan that defines the quality practices, resources and activities relevant to the devices that are being designed and manufactured at that facility. The firm needs to have written procedures that describe how they intend to meet their quality requirements.

For firms that manufacture devices as well as other products, there must be a quality plan that is specifically relevant to devices. Much of what is required to be part of the plan may be found in the firm's quality system documentation, such as, the Quality Manual, Device Master Record(s), production procedures, etc. Therefore, the plan itself may be a roadmap of the firm's quality system. The plan in this case would need to include reference to applicable quality system documents and how those documents apply to the device(s) that is the subject of the plan.

Quality plans may be specific to one device or be generic to all devices manufactured at the firm. Quality plans can also be specific to processes or overall systems.

All manufacturers of medical devices are required to establish and implement a quality system tailored to the device manufactured. Each manufacturer must prepare and implement all activities, including, but not necessarily limited to the applicable requirements of the Quality System Regulation, that are necessary to assure the finished device, the design process, the manufacturing process, and all related activities conform to approved specifications.

The term "quality system" as specified in the Quality System Regulation encompasses all activities previously referred to as "quality assurance" which were necessary to assure the finished device meets its predetermined design specifications. This includes assuring manufacturing processes are controlled and adequate for their intended use, documentation is controlled and maintained, equipment is calibrated, inspected, tested, etc. Some manufacturers may use the terms "quality control" or "GMP Control" or "quality assurance" instead of quality system. It doesn't matter what term is used as long as the quality system concept is understood and implemented.

Written quality system procedures and instructions are required. Any FDA 483 observation regarding Quality System procedures must be specific and point out the controls that are missing or believed inadequate.

Sample Warning Letters

1. **Failure to establish an adequate and effective quality system that has been fully implemented and maintained at all levels of the organization, as required by 21 C.F.R. 820.20 (a).** During the FDA inspection, we observed significant violations as they relate to a number of quality system requirements, including lack of a quality policy that is understood, implemented and maintained; lack of appointment of a management representative to oversee and maintain quality system; lack of management reviews of the quality system; and lack of a total quality plan which defines the quality practices.

2. **Failure to establish the appropriate responsibility, authority, and interrelation of all personnel who manage, perform, and assess work affecting quality, and provide the independence and authority necessary to perform these tasks, as required by 21 CFR 820.20(b)(1).** For example: Your firm's procedures list corporate entities, positions, and individuals which are not part of the firm's current corporate structure for quality; Your firm failed to list second shift quality personnel, their positions, and to whom they report within the corporate quality structure; Your firm's procedures fail to list the current individuals with responsibility and authority of management review.

3. **Failure of the management representative to ensure quality system requirements are**

effectively established and effectively maintained within the organization, as required by 21 CFR 820.20(b)(3)(i). For example, problems were noted with quality assurance, documentation, process controls, complaint handling, data analysis, employee training, and equipment maintenance at your facility that resulted in the development of the Process Validation Remediation Project Summary (Summary). This Summary described the firm's reengineered Quality System which was implemented in in 2006, and applies to all Arrow International manufacturing facilities. In 2007, the Management Representative stated that he had not seen the Summary. This Summary was sent to the FDA in December 2006 with a cover letter January 2007. The Summary was sent to two employees who reported to the Management Representative at the facility but apparently had not been provided to the Management Representative himself.

4. **Failure to establish procedures for management review as required by 21 CFR 820.20(c).** Specifically, there is no procedure established for conducting management reviews. In addition, no formal management reviews have been documented within the last three years.

5. **Failure to establish procedures to ensure management with executive responsibility review the suitability and effectiveness of the quality system at defined intervals and with sufficient frequency to ensure the quality system satisfies the requirements of 21 CFR Part 820 and the manufacturer's established quality**

policy and objectives, as required by 21 CFR 820.20(c). Specifically, your "Management review" procedure states that management review meetings are to be conducted annually. Per your CEO, your firm has not conduct a management review in the past 4 years.

6. **Failure to establish a quality plan, as required by 21 CFR 820.20(d).** For example, your SOPs were limited to laboratory operations and failed to cover/include, among other things, SOPs for management controls, corrective and preventive action, and handling nonconformance.

7. **Your firm failed to establish quality system procedures and instructions, as required by 21 CFR 820.20(e).** Specifically, your firm has no established procedures to ensure the quality system records associated with the acquired device to include device history records, drawings, specifications, procedures, etc., were received at the time of the acquisition.

D.G. Daugherty

5 QUALITY AUDIT

THE REGULATION

Subpart B—Quality System Requirements

820.22 Quality audit. Each manufacturer shall establish procedures for quality audits and conduct such audits to assure that the quality system is in compliance with the established quality system requirements and to determine the effectiveness of the quality system. Quality audits shall be conducted by individuals who do not have direct responsibility for the matters being audited. Corrective action(s), including a reaudit of deficient matters, shall be taken when necessary. A report of the results of each quality audit, and reaudit(s) where taken, shall be made and such reports shall be reviewed by management having responsibility for the matters audited. The dates and

results of quality audits and reaudits shall be documented.

Excerpts from the Preamble

Quality audits are for an internal audit and review of the quality system to verify compliance with the quality system regulation. The review and evaluations under section 820.22 are very focused. During the internal quality audit, the manufacturer should review all procedures to ensure adequacy and compliance with the regulation, and determine whether the procedures are being effectively implemented at all times.

In contrast, as noted above, the management review under section 820.20(c) is a broader review of the organization as a whole to ensure that the quality policy is implemented and the quality objectives are met. The reviews of the quality policy and objectives (section 820.20(c)) should be carried out by top management, and the review of supporting activities (section 820.22) should be carried out by management with executive responsibility for quality and other appropriate members of management, utilizing competent personnel as decided on by management.

Section 820.22 clarifies that a re-audit is not always required, but where it is indicated, it must be conducted. The report should verify that corrective action was implemented and effective. Because FDA does not review these reports, the date on which the audit and re-audit were performed must be documented and will be subject to

FDA review.

Quality System Inspection Technique Guide

Inspectional Objectives

Verify that quality audits, including re-audits of deficient matters, of the quality system are being conducted.

FDA reviews a firm's quality audit schedules to assure quality audits are being conducted with sufficient frequency. It is recommended that the time between quality audits not exceed a 12-month period. More frequent audits may be recommended if the firm has a serious QS Regulation problem.

Quality audits should consist of a formal, planned check of all elements in the quality system. They are NOT product audits. Quality audits must be conducted using adequate detailed written procedures by appropriately trained individuals. If conducted properly, a quality audit can detect system defects and, through isolation of unsatisfactory trends and correction of factors that cause defective products, prevent the production of unsafe or nonconforming devices. Without an effective quality audit function the quality system is incomplete and there is no assurance the manufacturer is consistently in a state-of-control.

Evidence of inadequate auditing may exist without gaining access to the written quality audit reports. This evidence may be obtained by relating the audit program to deficiencies observed in other subsystems. If significant quality system problems have existed both before and after the firm's last self-audit, then you should critically review the written audit procedures. The audit procedures should cover each quality system, and should be specific enough to enable the person conducting the audit to perform an adequate audit. The auditors must be adequately trained. If it is necessary and possible to interview an auditor, ask how the audits are performed; what documents are examined; how long audits take; etc.

Audits should be conducted by individuals not having direct responsibility for matters being audited. One person and other very small firms must generally establish independence, even if it means hiring outside auditors, because the failure to have an independent auditor could result in an ineffective audit. If there are significant FDA 483 observations, and independent audits are being performed, but deficiencies are apparently not being identified by the auditor, then an FDA 483 should contain an observation indicating a lack of adequate audits.

FDA will determine whether corrective action by upper management is being taken. Auditors may be asked if they observed any of the ongoing QS Regulation deficiencies during their prior audits (ongoing QS Regulation deficiencies may also be identified by reviewing prior FDA 483's). If the answer is yes, check the written audit schedule, if available, to determine if a follow up audit is scheduled for the deficient areas. Check the written audit procedure for instructions for review of audits by upper management. For example, do the procedures require quality audit results to be included in the management reviews? Verify that the procedures contain provisions for the re-audit of deficient areas if necessary. A failure to implement follow up corrective actions, including re-audits of deficient matters may be listed as a Quality System Regulation deficiency on the FDA 483.

NOTE: Re-audits of deficient matters are not always required, but where one is indicated, it must be conducted. The reaudit report should verify the recommended corrective action(s) was implemented and effective.

Sample Warning Letters

1. **Failure to establish procedures for quality audits as required by 21 CFR 820.22.** Specifically, there is no procedure established for conducting quality audits. In addition, there is no documentation that internal audits have been conducted within the last three years.

2. **Failure to establish a procedure for quality audits, and to conduct and document quality audits, as required by 21 CFR 820.22.** You do not conduct quality audits to assure the quality system is in compliance with the established quality system requirements and to determine the effectiveness of the quality system.

3. **Failure to establish procedures for quality audits and conduct such audits to assure that the quality system is in compliance with the established quality system requirements and to determine the effectiveness of the quality system, as required by 21 CFR 820.22.** For example: The procedure to conduct internal audits lacks instructions for reaudits of deficient matters, if necessary as required by regulation.

4. **Failure to establish and maintain adequate procedures for quality audits, as required by 21 CFR 820.22.** For example, your firm's quality audit procedure requires auditors to be independent. However:

   a. The Quality Manager, responsible for the oversight of equipment, audited the area "Equipment of measuring, checking, and testing."

   b. The Quality Manager Assistant audited the "Control of the electronic design." The Quality Manager Assistant conducted an audit in an area where they had responsibility.

   c. The Quality Manager Assistant audited the area –"Control of the electronic design." This individual does not have the adequate training or background to review firmware verification or validations.

6 PERSONNEL

THE REGULATION

820.25 Personnel.

(a) General. Each manufacturer shall have sufficient personnel with the necessary education, background, training, and experience to assure that all activities required by this part are correctly performed.

(b) Training. Each manufacturer shall establish procedures for identifying training needs and ensure that all personnel are trained to adequately perform their assigned responsibilities. Training shall be documented.

   (1) As part of their training, personnel shall be made aware of device defects which may occur from the improper performance

of their specific jobs.

(2) Personnel who perform verification and validation activities shall be made aware of defects and errors that may be encountered as part of their job functions.

<u>Excerpts from the Preamble</u>

Whether "sufficient" personnel are employed will be determined by the requirements of the quality system, which must be designed to ensure that the requirements of the regulation are properly implemented.

In making staffing decisions, a manufacturer must ensure that persons assigned to particular functions are properly equipped and possess the necessary education, background, training, and experience to perform their functions correctly.

FDA agrees that the manufacturer must determine for itself what constitutes "sufficient" personnel with proper qualification in the first instance. However, if the manufacturer does not employ sufficient personnel, or personnel with the necessary qualifications to carry out their functions, the manufacturer will be in violation of the regulation. FDA has often found that the failure to comply with this requirement leads to other significant regulatory violations.

Training procedure includes the identification of training needs. FDA notes, however, that a training program to ensure personnel adequately perform their assigned responsibilities should include information about the CGMP requirements and how particular job functions relate to the overall quality system.

FDA further believes that it is imperative that training cover the consequences of improper performance so that personnel will be apprised of defects that they should look for, as well as be aware of the effect their actions can have on the safety and effectiveness of the device.

In order for the full quality system to function as intended, all personnel should be properly trained. Each function in the manufacture of a medical device must be viewed as integral to all other functions.

Sample Warning Letters

1. **Failure to have sufficient personnel with the necessary education, background, training, and experience to assure that all activities required by 21 CFR 820 are correctly performed, as required by 21 CFR 820.25(a).** For example:

   a. The job description for the Director of Quality Systems requires that the person have a Bachelor of Science/Technical/or Engineering discipline. The person holding the position does not have this type of degree, but rather a Business Administration degree.

   b. The person holding the Regulatory Affairs Manager position lacks the minimum of 5 years of regulatory experience required in the job description.

c. The person holding the Quality Control Supervisor position lacks the required Bachelor degree in science or the alternative five to eight years of experience in Quality Control.

d. The person holding the Calibration Coordinator position lacks the required Bachelor degree and the four years of relevant experience.

2. **Personnel training is not documented, as required by 21 CFR 820.25(b).** Specifically, your firm does not have any personnel training records for the quality system standard operating procedures for which they are responsible.

3. **Failure to establish procedures for identifying training needs and ensure that all personnel are trained to adequately perform their assigned responsibilities, as required by 21 CFR 820.25(b).** For example:

a. The firm lacked documented evidence showing that the firm's employees, including the General Manager and Production Supervisor, have received formal training in Good Manufacturing Practices (GMP) as they apply to their specific tasks and the medical devices manufactured at the firm as required by the firm's procedure.

b. Upon request by the investigator, the firm was unable to provide documentation showing that personnel conducting the inspection of the sealed bags, containing the sterile culture media plates, have been trained to detect all possible defects that may be encountered affecting the packaging seal integrity.

4. **Failure to establish and maintain procedures for identifying training needs and ensure that all personnel are trained to adequately perform their assigned responsibilities, as required by 21 CFR 820.25 (b).** Specifically, your training program procedure is not being implemented in that there is no documented training for any of your firm's employees.

7 CONCLUSION

To reiterate, I wrote the *Practitioner's Guide to Management Controls* because it seems to me that many practitioners, particularly those new to medical devices, are sometimes overwhelmed by the QS Regulation requirements for management controls and how to interpret them. These practitioners may also not be aware of, or have access to, many of the resources available to the industry.

Having experienced the same challenges at times in my twenty five year medical device career, I determined that I would provide a concise, comprehensive, and affordable, collection of information pertaining to the QS Regulation that may prove helpful to these practitioners. This book, using essential information from FDA sources, provides essential information for practitioners particularly interested in the Management Controls subsystem.

The *Practitioner's Guide to Management Controls* provides important information to the practitioner that may enable them to better:

- Interpret the requirements for their firm

- Understand some of FDA's expectations for compliance

- Obtain awareness regarding how an firm is evaluated by the FDA for compliance, and

- See actions that have led to warning letters for compliance issues that were not suitably addressed

A practitioner should be able to see what is required and expected of their medical device firm by relating the specific requirements communicated in the regulation itself, along with the valuable information the FDA provided in the preamble regarding the intent of the regulation and expectations for firms in the medical device industry. Additionally, by reviewing the QSIT inspectional objectives and techniques, a practitioner will note how their firm may be evaluated during the course of a routine FDA inspection. This information should help the practitioner be prepared for an inspection by developing and maintaining a compliant quality system at all times. A review of sample warning letters should also provide insight to a practitioner when developing or improving their firm's quality system.

ABOUT THE AUTHOR

D.G. Daugherty is an accomplished medical device quality assurance professional with over 25 years of experience in quality engineering, management, and compliance with some of the world's largest medical device manufacturing companies. He is highly knowledgeable in requirements of FDA QSR 820, ISO 13485, and ISO 14971, manufacturing process validation (IQ, OQ, PQ), quality system development, Corrective and Preventive Action (CAPA), and quality performance metrics and analytics. He is exceptionally skilled in statistical techniques, process improvement, problem solving, and root cause analysis.

D.G. Daugherty is also a senior member of the American Society for Quality (ASQ) and maintains professional certifications through ASQ as a Certified Six Sigma Black Belt, Quality Engineer, and Quality Auditor.